THE MAGDALENE WOMEN

The Untold Story Of Ireland's Magdalene Laundries And How Thousands Of Women Vanished Behind Convent Walls.

Nutshell Nook

Table of Contents

Introduction

The unmarked graves of 155 nuns were discovered by construction workers at Dublin's High Park convent on a chilly February morning in 1993. This discovery would rock Ireland to its foundations. Within the confines of a Magdalene Laundry, these women had lived, worked, and passed away; their experiences were hidden behind decades of institutional silence, and their identities were only listed on shaky death certificates. A clear example of how totally these ladies had disappeared from public consciousness and official records is the fact that just 75 of them had valid death certificates.

Ireland has long chosen to deny its past, but the discovery compelled it to face it. An estimated 30,000 women have entered Ireland's Magdalene Laundries for more than 200 years. They were aunts and sisters, moms and daughters. Some joined at the age of fourteen, while others lived out the rest of their lives behind the tall stone walls that surrounded Ireland's cities. They cleaned and pressed linens at government offices, hotels, restaurants, and private residences while working in sweltering laundry facilities for no pay. They never received a dime of the profit that their efforts produced.

Although these establishments portrayed themselves as havens and havens for "fallen women," the truth was far more nuanced. Young women were incarcerated for a variety of reasons, from slight disobedience to rejection from family, from poverty to unmarried pregnancy. Some had aged out of industrial schools and were orphans. Some were sent by their own relatives, who saw them as an embarrassment. A shadow system of imprisonment that functioned outside of legal frameworks was established as a result of the referrals made by courts and governmental entities.

The last Magdalene Laundry in Ireland, located on Dublin's Sean McDermott Street, closed its doors in 1996. It continued to function well into the days of color television, low-cost airplanes, and the early internet, so it was neither a holdover from Victorian morality nor post-independence poverty. Dublin's streets were still populated with women who had worked there, silently bearing their memories. These institutions had survived till the end of the twentieth century in Ireland, a country that took pride in its Celtic Tiger economy and progressive social ideals.

The tales of the ladies came out slowly at first, then quickly. They related stories of terrible working conditions and chilly dorms, of names being substituted with numbers, and of unanswered letters home. They explained a kind of control that went beyond physical restraint and aimed to change who they were. In addition to being places of employment, they were also places of extreme seclusion where women were separated from their communities, families, and sense of self.

The actual structures are still standing in Irish cities. Others are still abandoned, with their vacant windows facing out into busy streets where people walk by unawares, while others have been transformed into offices or flats. These buildings in Cork, Limerick, Galway, and Dublin serve as tangible reminders of a system that functioned covertly and was maintained by an intricate network of governmental, ecclesiastical, and social collaboration.

Records show that Ireland's most esteemed establishments, including government agencies, colleges, and upscale hotels, shipped their laundry to these locations. They participated in an economy of exploitation that was legitimized by the rhetoric of social control and moral rehabilitation, profiting from the unpaid work of imprisoned women. Through agreements, recommendations, and tacit legal recognition, the state actively supported these institutions rather than playing a passive role.

The effects of their incarceration were felt long after they were released by the women who survived. Many suffered from social humiliation, financial difficulty, and psychological suffering. Some left their home countries, bringing with them their unwritten histories. Others stayed in Ireland, living close to the identical institutions that had imprisoned them, their quiet compelled by social disinterest and embarrassment. Generation after generation was affected: communities characterized by unspoken knowledge, families shattered by concealment, and children torn away from their mothers.

There is more to the history of Ireland's Magdalene Laundries than meets the eye. It brings up pressing issues about social control, institutional authority, and how disadvantaged groups are treated. It exposes how exploitation and incarceration systems may endure in countries that seem to be progressing, challenging cozy myths about modernity and development. Above all, it serves as evidence of the tenacity of women who overcame these establishments and ultimately discovered the courage to express their opinions.

Former prisoners faced both public incredulity and official opposition as they organized and pushed for recognition. How long have these institutions been in place? How would society have permitted this to occur? Examining the intricate relationships between state power, church authority, and societal perceptions of women's autonomy and sexuality holds the key to the solutions. Recognizing this history necessitates facing up to difficult realities regarding shared accountability and the fallout from institutional abuse.

The 1993 discovery of those unmarked graves sparked a national reckoning that is still going on today. The women who went through the Magdalene Laundries were not merely victims of a system that was out of date; rather, they were people whose lives were drastically changed by an establishment that functioned with broad social approval. Their stories highlight important realities about gender, power, and the cost of conformity in contemporary Ireland.

Chapter 1

Origins

A structure that would influence Irish society for more than 200 years began in 1765 when Lady Arabella Denny founded the Dublin Magdalen Asylum on Lower Leeson Street. Her Protestant organization, which operated on the tenets of Christian charity and moral reform that mirrored the social standards of Georgian Dublin, exclusively took Protestant women. Upon entering, the women were immersed in a world of rigorous routine, prayer, and what the institution's founders referred to as "purposeful work."

Patterns that would subsequently spread across Ireland were established in the early years of the Dublin asylum. In order to inculcate discipline and morality, the founders of the institution felt that Lady Denny's model placed a strong emphasis on religious education in addition to labor, especially laundry work. Laundry labor was chosen because it symbolized the washing away of sin through hard effort. Later on, the whole network of Magdalene institutions across Ireland would be infused with this iconography.

However, what started out as a Protestant project quickly changed. The asylum concept was adopted and adapted by Catholic religious organizations as they became more prominent in Ireland throughout the nineteenth century. Their organizations were quite different from what Lady Denny had in mind. More severe settings were established by the Catholic orders, which prioritized penance above recovery. They quickly grew, setting up shop in numerous smaller towns as well as all of Ireland's main cities.

The main organizations that ran these facilities were the Sisters of Mercy, the Sisters of Our Lady of Charity, and the Religious Sisters of Charity. Their expanding network was a reflection of the Catholic Church's rising social influence in Ireland as well as the nuanced interplay between social control and religious authority. These orders operated as part of a larger system that also included mother and infant homes, industrial schools, and other establishments aimed at dealing with what society considered to be moral breaches.

Deeper shifts in Irish society were mirrored in the conversion from a Protestant charity to a Catholic one. Operating under its Protestant ethos until 1994, the original Dublin institution relocated to Eglinton Road, Donnybrook, in 1959. Catholic-run institutions, on the other hand, grew and created a network that lasted until 1996. The Catholic Church's increasing control over Irish social services and its function in establishing moral standards were reflected in this development.

In the late eighteenth century, the phrase "fallen women" was first used to refer to sex workers, although its definition changed significantly throughout time. Women who had never worked in sex were confined in the Magdalene laundries during the late nineteenth century. When women questioned or fell short of society's moral standards, the institutions became catch-alls. These establishments may be the destination for young ladies who were deemed "too pretty" or "flirtatious" by local priests or police. Orphans, rape victims, unmarried moms, and women deemed "simple" or "troubled" were all included in the expanding list of those who needed the laundries' "protection."

Many of the agreements made at that time were arbitrary, according to historical records. Because of her family's inability to provide for her, the perception that she was too beautiful and hence "in moral danger," or the fact that she had no other choice in a culture that gave women little economic autonomy, a woman may go into the sewing shop. Entries for "incompetent," "simple," "troubled," and other ambiguous labels that concealed intricate social and economic constraints may be found in the institutions' registry.

These institutions' development was a reflection of larger socio economic dynamics in Irish society. Together with other Catholic-run establishments, the laundromats evolved into tools of social control as the Catholic Church solidified its hold on power in the nineteenth century. Through police collaboration, court referrals, and ultimately, commercial washing service contracts, the state implicitly supported this system.

Economic realities were hidden by the religious explanations. Operating on unpaid labor, the laundromats catered to both private clients and government contracts. Long after their initial social goal had been lost, this economic model made sure they would continue. The institutions that imprisoned the women were funded in part by their unpaid labor, resulting in a self-sustaining system that lasted long into the twentieth century.

The change was finished by the late nineteenth century. Lady Denny's Protestant charity project had developed into a national network of Catholic organizations that combined social control, economic exploitation, and religious authority. Irish society was able to conceal its unpleasant realities—poverty, unmarried motherhood, dysfunctional families, and the effects of sexual abuse—in the laundries. Behind lofty walls and institutional quiet, the women within vanished, their efforts removing the filth of others while their own experiences went unheard.

Information regarding their activities was strictly controlled by the religious orders. Later, attempts to fully comprehend the laundries' influence on Irish society would be hampered by this concealment. The documents that have survived depict organizations that expanded much beyond their initial purpose and became a vital component of Ireland's social fabric. When the registers of the religious orders are accessible, they show hundreds of women who have gone through the system; each record reflects a life that was disrupted, redirected, or irrevocably changed by their stay inside the walls of the laundries.

Chapter 2

Life Inside

With finality, the iron gates closed behind them. That sound signaled the start of a new life for hundreds of Irish women who worked in Magdalene Laundries between 1765 and 1996. At six in the morning, the sound of the morning bell reverberated through the stone hallways. Silently, women got out of their little mattresses and walked to unheated chapels for morning prayers. Names were removed, and "house names"—often the names of saints—were given in their stead, destroying personal identities.

The strict framework that governed each hour is recalled by Mary Norris, who entered in 1964: "You weren't allowed to talk to anyone." We even ate breakfast in total silence while a nun read aloud from sacred books. Bread and light porridge were the usual morning fare. All of the ladies were supposed to be at their washing stations by 7 AM.

Ireland's institutions were fueled by large-scale washing businesses. These establishments received linens from private residences, hotels, hospitals, and government buildings. Women handled toxic chemicals and boiling water without safety gear while working for no compensation. Steam and the pungent odor of bleach filled the air as the machines thundered continuously. Burns were frequent. As women stood for hours at ironing boards, pushed sheets through mangles, and hoisted heavy, damp linens, the physical toll increased.

Catherine McGuinness, a former resident, explained the ongoing strain: "The labor never ended. They would yell that you were lazy and that this was God's way of punishing you for your transgressions if you slowed down. The hot water and chemicals would cause your hands to break and bleed, but you were powerless to stop it. With only short intervals for meals—always consumed in strict silence—the labor went on until six o'clock in the afternoon.

Control was not limited to the physical world. Family letters were read and edited. Many ladies were unaware of whether their letters were received at home. Visits were either prohibited or severely limited. Behind tall walls and barred gates, the outside world vanished. Upon entrance, personal belongings were seized. Even little displays of individuality were punished.

"If you spoke during meals, you'd be made to kneel for hours," recalls Elizabeth Manning, who worked in a Dublin laundry for three years. If they believed you to be conceited, they would chop your hair short. The heads of a few females who attempted to flee were entirely shaved. Reductions in food rations, longer workdays, and seclusion in "locks"—small, dim rooms—were among the penalties.

Every spare minute was filled with religious teaching. Women had to offer up prayers for their "sins" all day long. The message was consistent: people needed to be redeemed by prayer and hard effort since they were fallen and undeserving. For decades after its distribution, many people carried the humiliation of having profoundly absorbed this message.

The evenings provided little respite. Spartan dorms had scant bedding and round-the-clock security.

"You couldn't even whisper to the girl in the next bed," remembers Sarah O'Connor, who was hospitalized in 1973 at the age of 16. Nuns were on patrol with spotlights all night long. They would punish you the next day if they caught you chatting.

There was little medical attention. It was common to accuse women of pretending to be unwell in order to avoid going to work. Recalling giving birth at a Magdalene laundry, Josephine McCarthy says, "There was no doctor, no pain relief." Then they took my baby away. I never had the opportunity to hold him. "They said I had to put in more hours to make up for the 'trouble' I had caused."

The psychological effects of this setting were disastrous. Women were informed they were useless outside the facility and that their family had abandoned them. "You lost yourself in there," said Martha Wilson, who spent 40 years in a Magdalene laundry after entering at the age of 15. You eventually began to believe what they were saying about you. Decades later, I still sometimes wake up to the voices telling me I'm nothing.

Using unpaid labor, the laundromats functioned as closed systems. The religious organizations got the profits from the washing job, but the women who produced this revenue were never paid. The Irish government is implicated in this system of forced labor, according to records that reveal significant contracts with state institutions, such as government offices and hospitals.

Survivors' bodies bear the physical scars of these years: respiratory disorders brought on by years of breathing in steam and bleach fumes, scarred hands from chemical burns, and persistent back problems from hard lifting. However, the unseen wounds are more profound. As a young nun at a Magdalene Laundry, Patricia Burke Brogan subsequently wrote: "The worst violence was the silence - the suppression of voices, of names, of stories." Souls were being crushed in addition to bodies being imprisoned.

The regular activities of the laundromats have a greater function: the methodical destruction of personal identity. From the wake-up bell to the lights-out, every element of life inside served to emphasize the idea that these women were there only for work and penance. Their testimonies, which surfaced decades later, highlight the significant human cost of this establishment that combined economic exploitation, social control, and religious authority.

These stories, which are gathered from survivors who have spoken their experiences in public, provide insight into a world that many Irish residents were unaware existed beyond their towns' high walls. Some survivors have found the courage to tell their story, while others have taken their experiences to the afterlife, leaving us with unanswered questions.

Chapter 3

The System at Work

There was much more to the Irish state's participation in the Magdalene Laundries than just knowledge. Women were aggressively directed to these colleges by government agencies, which also offered them lucrative contracts. Despite Dáil worries about job losses in the legal laundry industry, the Irish army conducted a deliberate transition from commercial laundries to these institutional enterprises in the early 1940s. When asked about this choice, Defense Minister Oscar Traynor said the contracts included "fair wages clauses"—a remark that seemed implausible considering that the women who performed this labor were never paid.

These institutions' whole economic model was predicated on unpaid forced labor. Women labored under difficult circumstances six days a week, often putting in over twelve hours a day. Carrying heavy, wet linens, running hazardous equipment, and working with caustic cleaning agents without safety gear made the job physically taxing. Everything from military clothes to clergy vestments, from hospital linens to hotel bedding, was washed and pressed by these ladies.

The most well-known institutions in Ireland were among the long list of clients that were discovered in 2011 in documents. Customers included the Irish president's official house, Áras an Uachtaráin. This exploitative structure benefitted the Bank of Ireland, Guinness Brewery, and important government agencies including Agriculture, Fisheries, and Defense. These services were employed by prestigious hotels, golf courses, and even the Gaiety Theatre, establishing a network of business ties that made the abuse seem commonplace.

The religious organizations that oversaw these establishments kept meticulous accounting records, meticulously recording all of their earnings and outlays. However, the women whose labor produced these earnings received no compensation. The ladies did not get any pension benefits, social insurance payments, or recognition for their labor. The orders amassed significant cash reserves as a result of their work, which was disguised as penance and rehabilitation.

A deeper cooperation was shown by the way the state and church operated these institutions. Although there was no legal basis for such operations, courts assigned women to the laundries as an alternative to jail terms. Women deemed "at risk" or "troublesome" were hauled to the laundries' doors by social workers and police. During their visit, government inspectors concentrated on the facilities' cleanliness and operational effectiveness, never raising concerns about the basic rights abuses taking place there.

Although each religious order had a distinct approach to their position, they all used similar methods of monitoring and control. Strict routines were followed by the Sisters of Mercy, Sisters of Our Lady of Charity, and Religious Sisters of Charity. Women were denied personal belongings, given religious names, and prohibited from speaking while at work. They had their correspondence read, their freedom of movement curtailed, and their access to the outside world severely curtailed.

The orders used a sophisticated theology of work-based atonement to defend their behavior. Although their techniques mirrored deeper currents of societal control and economic exploitation, they saw themselves as providing shelter and reformation to "fallen women." The nuns in charge of the laundromats lived apart from the penitents, ate different foods, and had access to advantages that the women under their supervision did not.

A focus on financial issues rather than pastoral care is seen in internal papers from different orders. Monthly reports kept careful tabs on washing business revenue, but expenditures for the imprisoned women were kept to a minimum. While women wore donated clothing and lived on meager rations, the orders made investments in expanding their buildings and equipment.

An analysis of state documents reveals the scope of this operation. Large amounts of money were paid to these establishments, according to government agencies' thorough records of their laundry expenses. Numerous laundromats nationwide were able to generate consistent revenue streams just on military contracts. Church and state were mutually dependent as a result of this financial arrangement, which supported the regime.

The laundries' ability to undercut commercial rivals who were required to provide basic working conditions and pay salaries was essential to their financial success. Businesses were forced to utilize institutional laundromats or found it difficult to compete with their artificially cheap pricing as a result of this unbalanced market. Even for free workers, the impact suppressed pay and working conditions as it spread across the legal laundry industry.

Former prisoners have explained how the religious groups used a mix of physical and psychological punishment to keep the peace. Women who did not fulfill their work quotas were punished by having their food rations cut, being confined in isolation, or having to do more work. The sisters persuaded many women that they were deserving of their treatment and captivity by using religious guilt and humiliation as methods of control.

The function of the state extends to the control architecture itself. Gardaí would aggressively look for women who had fled and bring them back to the facilities. Health inspectors ignored infractions of fundamental safety and sanitary regulations. Politicians avoided discussing the circumstances at the laundromats, citing the church's social authority instead.

Because it catered to many interests at once, this system endured. The state maintained a practical answer for "problem" women while saving money on institutional laundry services. The church made a substantial profit while expanding its social influence. Low-cost services were provided to businesses without requiring them to consider the human cost. Because their work was done behind towering barriers that prevented them from being seen by the public, the women themselves continued to have no voice.

The 1993 discovery at Dublin's High Park Convent made the system's significant economic effect abundantly evident. Women buried on the site were exhumed by the Sisters of Our Lady of Charity when they had to sell the land to pay for financial losses. As they looked for the most cost-effective way to relocate these unmarked graves, the sisters' attention to detail continued after death. This episode revealed the system's profoundly commercial character in addition to its human cost.

Chapter 4

Breaking Silence

Everything changed in the spring of 1993. Something surprising was hit by the equipment used by construction workers on a plot of land in High Park, Drumcondra. In order to offset losses from failed stock market investments, the Sisters of Our Lady of Charity sold a portion of their convent grounds to a real estate developer. Rather, this corporate choice revealed a wealth of information that had been kept hidden for many years.

The tale that came out of the earth was one that the country was not ready to hear. Unmarked and unreported, the workmen had found a mass burial. Many of the 155 women whose remains were buried had no identities, no death certificates, and no formal documentation of their demise. Their revelation would rock Ireland to its core; these were the forgotten women of the Magdalene Laundries.

The sum of the numbers was off. Although 155 remains were discovered, the Sisters had only obtained permission to exhume 133. Only 75 of them received death certificates, which is a glaring disregard for Irish law, which mandates that all fatalities on institutional property be reported. The religious order came up with a quick and contentious solution: they shared the expenses with the property developer to have the corpses cremated and reburied in a mass grave in Glasnevin Cemetery.

As so many things had been in the past, the finding may have remained a quiet scandal, handled quietly between local politicians and church authorities. However, Ireland was evolving. Reporters started to inquire. After decades of keeping their experiences hidden, survivors began to come up. After more than two centuries of protection, the wall of silence that surrounded the Magdalene Laundries started to crumble.

"Sex in a Cold Climate" on Channel 4 featured the first significant public accounts of Magdalene survivors in 1997. After years of quiet, Mary Norris, Josephine McCarthy, and Mary-Jo McDonagh finally spoke about their experiences. Their descriptions of life in the laundromats ran counter to the official narrative of philanthropic organizations assisting "fallen women." They described life being snatched, punishment, loneliness, and continuous unpaid labor.

In Britain and Ireland, millions of people watched the documentary. Its influence spread across Irish culture, resulting in awkward discussions in bars, homes, and finally government buildings. Too many women were coming out with identical allegations, so they couldn't be written off as isolated events or exaggerations.

"The Magdalene Sisters" by Peter Mullan, released in 2002, turned these testimonials into a story that appealed to viewers throughout the world. The video, which was based on victim testimonies, exposed the terrible reality of life inside the laundromats and peeled away the sanitized version of history. It raised awareness of Ireland's secret past on a worldwide scale and took home the Golden Lion at the Venice Film Festival.

The documentary "The Forgotten Maggies" by Steven O'Riordan gave the public record important new perspectives. Through his efforts, a ledger revealing the level of institutional participation with the laundries was discovered. Áras an Uachtaráin, Guinness, Clerys, the Gaiety Theatre, Dr. Steevens' Hospital, the Bank of Ireland, government agencies, golf clubs, and prestigious hotels were among the names in that ledger, which read like a who's who of Irish society. This was not a side business; rather, it was an integral part of Irish social and economic life.

When the program aired on TG4 in 2011, more than 360,000 people watched it. More importantly, it encouraged a lot more survivors to come forward. For the first time, these women banded together to seek justice and acknowledgment, forming a new advocacy organization called Magdalene Survivors Together. The first Magdalene survivors to meet with Irish government representatives were the women shown in O'Riordan's documentary.

More information concerning the state's extensive participation with the laundries surfaced as media scrutiny grew. According to Mary Raftery's 2011 study in The Irish Times, state institutions purposefully transferred their laundry contracts from commercial operations to the Magdalene institutions in the early 1940s. Notwithstanding the Dáil's worries on employment losses in commercial laundromats, this business transfer took place. Oscar Traynor, the defense minister at the time, had said that these contracts had "fair wages clauses"—a bitter irony considering that the ladies were paid nothing.

The disclosures continued. An advocacy organization called Justice for Magdalenes gathered sufficient proof of human rights abuses to present their case before the UN Committee Against Torture. In their presentation, they described decades of psychological torture, forced incarceration, and unpaid work. The UN committee's answer was clear: Ireland has to look into these decades-old claims of torture.

Pressure for government action increased with each new piece of evidence, victim testimonies, documentary, and news story. The unmarked graves in High Park had given rise to tales that could no longer be buried. The long-suppressed women's voices were finally heard by a media that was willing to pay attention. In the end, a state inquiry that confirmed what survivors had been saying for years—that the Magdalene Laundries constituted a systemic failure of Irish society to protect its most vulnerable citizens—was brought about by the effect of these discoveries, which forced Ireland to face its history.

Chapter 5

Justice and Recognition

The women of Ireland's Magdalene Laundries kept their tails to themselves for decades. Everything changed in 1993 when 155 unmarked graves were found on the grounds of the High Park convent. Public indignation was sparked by this finding, which set off a series of events that would make Ireland confront its history.

The first reaction from the Irish government was insufficient. Testimonies from survivors surfaced via media coverage and films throughout the 1990s and early 2000s, but government action was still little. When the advocacy group Justice for Magdalenes took their case to the UN Committee Against Torture in 2011, it marked a sea change. Human rights abuses inside the laundries' walls were vividly shown in their presentation. The Irish government was eventually forced to take action when the UN committee made an urgent request for a probe.

What followed was an 18-month investigation headed by Senator Martin McAleese. The first thorough analysis of state participation in the Magdalene system was the result of his committee's work. Deep state involvement was shown by the results, which were released in February 2013. Since Ireland gained her independence in 1922, more than 11,000 women have enrolled at these institutions. The laundries received a lot of business from government contracts. Women were aggressively directed to these institutions by state authorities. Although there was no evidence of frequent physical or sexual assault, the investigation identified a lot of verbal abuse, a finding that several survivors disagreed with.

On February 19, 2013, the most important formal recognition day occurred. Many people believed they would never hear Taoiseach Enda Kenny's speech when he stood in front of Dáil Éireann. "I, as Taoiseach, on behalf of the State, the government and our citizens deeply regret and apologize unreservedly to all those women for the hurt that was done to them, and for any stigma they suffered, as a result of the time they spent in a Magdalene Laundry." Kenny spoke passionately when he called the laundromat "the nation's shame." For a large number of survivors in the public gallery, these remarks were the first formal recognition of their pain.

However, decades of unpaid work and lost lives could not be addressed by apologies alone. In order to define criteria for payouts and support services, the government appointed Judge John Quirke to oversee the compensation plan. 814 survivors received €32.8 million from the program by 2022. But this procedure led to new conflicts. The government and the UN repeatedly pleaded with the religious organizations that operated the laundries to pay to the reparations fund, but they refused.

The compensation plan itself turned out to be contentious. The application procedure, which required survivors to verify their experience in facilities with sometimes destroyed or incomplete records, was painful for many of them. Some women found it difficult to use the program, especially those who had immigrated to the UK or another country. Others said the rewards, which ranged from €11,500 for women who worked in a laundry for three months or less to €100,000 for those who worked there for ten years or more, were insufficient recompense for years of unpaid labor and lost independence.

Slowly, tangible memorials began to appear. Plans to convert the Sean McDermott Street building, the location of Ireland's last Magdalene laundry, into a monument and research center were authorized by Dublin City Council in 2022. In the same year, survivors came together to unveil the Journey Stone monument at St. Stephen's Green. The memorial's unique value, according to one survivor, stems from the fact that survivors themselves were involved in its conception and design, in contrast to previous commemorative initiatives.

The path of reconciliation was hampered by the religious organizations' reaction to demands for justice. Two unnamed religious sisters defended their organizations in a 2013 radio appearance, saying they had rendered a "free service for the country" and declining to offer an apology. This position brought attention to the ongoing discrepancy between institutional viewpoints and the experiences of survivors. Even though some 600 survivors were still living in 2014, the Sisters of

Mercy, Sisters of Our Lady of Charity of the Good Shepherd, and Religious Sisters of Charity continued to oppose monetary contributions to the compensation plan.

Preservation attempts encountered difficulties. Before their historical value could be preserved, several previous laundry locations were developed or demolished. Survivors' access to their own history was restricted since records were either destroyed or kept secret. However, grassroots initiatives to record and preserve the accounts of survivors arose. Testimonies were recorded for oral history initiatives. Scholars looked over the documents that were accessible. Commemorative activities were planned by community organizations.

The pursuit of justice exposed more general trends in the way Irish society views its history. Decisions made by local authorities sometimes seemed to be unrelated to initiatives for national recognition. For instance, in Ennis, the town council honored the Sisters of Mercy by renaming a road that passes past a former laundry site "Bóthar na Trócaire" (Road of Compassion). This move generated discussion on how communities should commemorate these establishments.

Pressure for accountability increased as a result of international attention. The religious orders were constantly asked to pay to reparation by the UN Committee on the Rights of the Child and Committee Against Torture. These foreign contributions demonstrated the resonance of Ireland's Magdalene experience with concerns about human rights and institutional abuse throughout the world.

Beyond political or historical ramifications, every step toward justice had personal importance for the remaining Magdalene women. After decades of quiet, several people spoke of feeling heard at last. Others had conflicting feelings, including persistent grief that no apology or money could completely alleviate and happiness at formal acknowledgment. Their ongoing support highlighted the fact that justice is still a work in progress rather than a finished product.

Chapter 6

Aftermath and Legacy

Mary Collins holds the Journey Stone monument in her palm as she stands in Dublin's St. Stephen's Green. "Every woman who walked through those gates lost something that can never be returned," she continues. Hundreds of survivors still talk about their experiences at Ireland's Magdalene Laundries, and her comments reflect their feelings. Once muffled behind institutional walls, their voices are now heard in government buildings, on media outlets, and in the minds of Irish people as a whole.

As they struggle for their current needs, the survivors who come forward now create vivid portraits of their prior experiences. "We were young when they took our health with the harsh chemicals and endless hours of laundry work," says Catherine Whelan, who is now in her seventies, describing the continuous battle for medical treatment. We need help now more than ever because we are elderly. Many survivors deal with comparable issues, such as physical problems brought on by years of taxing work, psychological trauma that shows itself in unexpected ways, and practical difficulty getting the promised recompense.

814 survivors have received €32.8 million from the compensation plan, which was put in place after the state's 2013 apologies. However, this number only accounts for a small portion of the 30,000 women who are thought to have visited the laundromats. Many survivors have lost their lives while awaiting acknowledgement. Others find it difficult to verify their imprisonment via the official procedures, particularly in light of the religious orders' ongoing resistance to disclosing information.

Despite repeated requests from the Irish government and UN committees, the Sisters of Mercy, Sisters of Our Lady of Charity of the Good Shepherd, and Religious Sisters of Charity have all declined to make contributions to the reparations fund. The profit these organizations made from decades of unpaid work contrasts sharply with their unwillingness. The cruel irony that some of the buildings where they used to labor for no pay have been sold for millions of euros, with none of the money raised going to help survivors, is noted by former inhabitants.

The fight for justice goes beyond monetary reparations. The right to recover personal histories, accurate identification of women in mass graves, and complete access to documents are demands made by survivors and their supporters. Although there was immediate outcry over the finding of 155 unmarked graves at High Park, comparable sites around Ireland have not been explored. A lady whose story has not been shared and whose family may still be looking for answers is symbolized by each unmarked grave.

Ireland now struggles in complex ways with this heritage. In order to educate young Irish people about this sad period of their history, the school curriculum now contains lessons on the Magdalene Laundries. However, there are still some communities who struggle with how to honor these locations. When local officials renamed a roadway in Ennis "Bóthar na Trócaire" (Road of Compassion) in honor of the Sisters of Mercy, the same order that operated the neighborhood laundry, controversy broke out. Survivors objected to this choice because they saw it as an effort to change history rather than face it head-on.

A step toward appropriate memory has been taken with the 2022 decision to turn the Sean McDermott Street laundry, the last to shut in 1996, into a monument and research center. Margaret O'Connor and other survivors, however, have conflicting opinions: "They're making judgments about our past without consulting us. We experienced it. We ought to be able to influence how it is remembered.

The Magdalene Laundries have a significant influence on modern Irish culture that goes far beyond their boundaries. These establishments represented a social control structure that influenced morality, sexuality, and women's views. Their legacy has an impact on current discussions in Ireland on women's rights, institutional accountability, and church-state ties.

Survivors have written more memoirs, oral histories, and creative works on their experiences in recent years. These testimonials are important historical documents as well as personal catharsis. They question the long-standing government narratives and enforced silence surrounding the laundries. In 2021, Mary Merritt, who became pregnant at the age of sixteen and lived in a laundry for years, released her story. "Every time one of us speaks," she continues, "we speak for all the women who never got the chance."

Irish policy debates concerning women's rights, church-state ties, and institutional care are still influenced by the experiences of Magdalene survivors. Advocates often cite the Magdalene Laundries as proof of how institutional abuse can thrive under government neglect when discussions about contemporary institutions—from direct provision centers to mental health facilities—occur.

Ireland's perception of its history and duty to its people has been profoundly changed by the women's fight for justice. Their tenacity undermined cozy national myths, prompted government probes, and garnered worldwide notice. Elizabeth Harrison, a survivor, states: "Ireland wanted to forget us." We refused to let them. They now have to recall not only what was done to us, but also how long it took them to admit it.

A rising number of young Irish activists relate the Magdalene Laundries' history to current battles for institutional accountability and women's rights. In order to make sure that this past influences Ireland's future, they research victim testimonials and assist current efforts. "The women of the laundries show us why we can never stop fighting for justice," said a young organizer at a recent memorial ceremony. As long as survivors continue to want acknowledgment and religious organizations continue to keep their secrets, their narrative is far from over.

Physical traces of the laundries may still be seen all throughout Ireland in the form of massive structures that have been abandoned or repurposed from housing hundreds of women and girls. Every location has a dilemma: how to accept previous transgressions while pursuing reconciliation. While some survivors support the buildings' preservation as historical landmarks, others want them to be dismantled because they perceive them as an unpleasant reminder of the tragedy.

At memory gatherings, former laundry workers often get together to encourage one another and share their stories with the next generation. Their testimonies are a powerful reminder of human tenacity and historical injustice. Once modest and clandestine, these events now get governmental acknowledgment and public attention. However, the most significant moments for many survivors occur during private discussions in which they share memories that only other survivors can fully comprehend.